CREATIVE TINY HANDS

Home and School

Creative activities for early childhood education

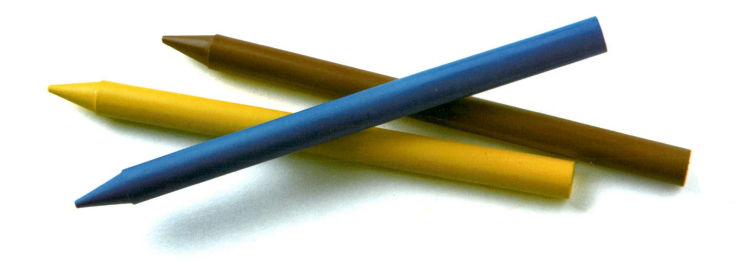

Home and School

Editorial Director: Mª Fernanda Canal
Editor: Jesús Araújo
Text and exercises: Anna Galera Bassachs,
Mònica Martí i Garbayo and Isabel Sanz Muelas
Series design: Toni Inglès
Graphic design and layout: Jordi Martínez
Photography: Nos & Soto, Index
Illustrations: Francesc Ràfols

First Published: April 2001
© Parramón Ediciones, S.A. - 2000. World rights
Published and distributed by Parramón Ediciones, S.A.
© Copyright of English edition for the United States its
territories and possessions including Puerto Rico
by Parramón Ediciones S.A. - Grupo Editorial Norma, 2001

ISBN: 84-342-2416-X
Printed in Spain

Complete or partial reproduction of this work by any means
or process, including printing, photocopying, microfilm,
scanning or any other system is forbidden without the written
permission of the publisher.

CONTENTS

4 Introduction
5 Techniques used
6 Methodological guidelines
7 Organization of the book
7 Home and School

8 The Range

10 The Slide

12 The Bed

14 The Pencil

16 The Clock

18 The Shower

20 The Backpack

22 The Washing Machine

24 The Ball

26 The House in the Mountains

28 The Block of Flats

30 The Doll

32 The Sink

34 The Smock

36 The Armchair

38 The "Tunnel"

40 The Country House

42 Templates

 # INTRODUCTION

The five volumes in the series CREATIVE TINY HANDS are aimed at pre-school children. The exercises contained in them are based on the subject matter of the different areas of the curriculum that are covered during this phase: learning about oneself and about one's natural and social environment. All the learning activities during this phase of learning center on these subjects. For this reason, this book contains strategies and resources that are highly useful for developing artistic expression that is both varied and motivating for children, and which aims to be innovative for adults.

We believe that there is nothing more useful for educators than to have access to new, original suggestions related to the subject matter that they are using in class at any given time, allowing children to do things, try things out and enjoy using different techniques, acquiring as they do so dexterity and confidence, and being as autonomous as possible. This collection will act as an excellent resource because it aims to be useful and functional for adults working with children of this age group, allowing them to refer to it in search of additional resources that complement each of the subjects they are dealing with.

Artistic language in the Second Cycle of Infant Education

Pre-school children are curious to discover and learn about everything that surrounds them, and to develop their thought processes through meaningful learning. In other words, learning that can be easily understood so that the child can relate what is already known to the new information. This type of learning allows the child to become familiar with, interpret, use and value reality. To aid this process, the activities suggested in this book have a global focus.

What does having a global focus mean? The child can not isolate one part from the whole, can not extract a single piece of information from its context. Instead he or she perceives different stimuli and sensations at the same time. The educator must have different tools and strategies at his or her disposal in order to be able to relate each artistic activity with areas of the curriculum. During this stage, cognitive activity must be stimulated by means of direct observation, interaction and experimentation. In the following suggested tasks, we aim to make the child use the process of discovery as a means of establishing new areas of learning. Artistic creation is involved in all educational processes, in all areas and everyday situations, and is an excellent means of expression.

Techniques used

The techniques found in this book for children to work with using their hands and experimenting are the ones that are most commonly used by this age group.

Punching: Use a felt mat and a punch. The child has to punch a series of holes along the line in order to be able to extract a shape that has already been drawn, without scraping the punch, and without ripping or tearing the paper with his or her fingers. A punch can also be used for making holes in the cardboard and inserting split pins.

Cutting: They should take the scissors in one hand and hold the paper up in the other hand to guide the movement of the scissors and follow the line.

Sticking: They should spread the correct amount of glue, bearing in mind the surface area being covered (if a large area is being glued, the glue will be spread over it and the material placed on top; on the other hand if it is a small area, the material will be placed on the stick of glue and then stuck in place.) The child must take care not to dirty either his or her hands or the table.

Tearing by hand: This should be done with two fingers making a "pincer", without tearing the paper at all.

Modeling plasticine: For covering large areas, it is necessary to roll out a piece of plasticine and spread it out with a thumb. When modeling small areas for decoration, you have to press it onto the cardboard to make it stick. It is always necessary to varnish the plasticine, to make it stick more strongly and to make it shiny and hard.

Modeling clay: First you have to knead the clay well with your hands to get rid of the air inside it, so that it does not crack as it dries. It is important to use a little water to join different pieces together, to cover cracks and to give a smooth finish. It is a good idea to paint or varnish the clay once it is dry, to give it a perfect finish.

Painting: This can be done with wax crayons, plastic crayons or felt-tipped pens. When using felt-tipped pens, they should not press too hard, to avoid flattening the point. When putting the lids on, make sure they are pressed on properly, so that the ink does not dry. You can also use paint (applied with fingers, hands or paintbrushes). When using a paintbrush, drain off excess paint, to avoid smudging or forming lumps. The paintbrush should be held lightly around the middle of the stick (not like a pencil) to paint with the brush part and without letting the stick scrape against the paper. They should spread the paint from top to bottom, and avoid circular movements.

Printing: Use different materials (potatoes, sponges, corks, parts of the body, etc.) To dip any of these materials into the paint, it is useful to use a sponge placed in a container full of paint diluted in water, so that the object is covered in the correct amount of paint.

Collage: Use different materials (clothing, paper of different textures and colors, stickers in different colors and shapes, wool, toothpicks, beans, pasta, coffee, beans, etc.)

Making windows: use cellophane, glossy paper, tissue paper, aluminum foil or crepe paper. The glue should always be spread around the hole in the cardboard from behind and the paper then stuck on, to prevent the paper getting dirty or creased.

Making balls: Use tissue paper, toilet paper, aluminum foil or other types of paper. Tear the paper and crumple it into a ball with the tips of the fingers. Using this technique stimulates fine motor skills by having to make a "pincer" with the fingers (forefinger and thumb.) When gluing the balls, spread the glue over the surface of the paper and then stick the balls to it. If it is a small area being stuck, rub the ball over the stick of glue and then stick it in place.

Making rolls: Use tissue paper, foil or plasticine. To make rolls with paper you have to press and roll the strip strongly with your fingers to achieve the shape and thickness you want.

Varnishing: Tissue paper, plasticine, wax crayons, beans, pasta, salt, sawdust and other materials. It will be necessary to varnish all these materials so that they remain fixed in place and bright. The children should use the correct width paintbrush so that they do not go beyond the area being varnished. Make sure that not too much varnish is used when covering flat surfaces, but in the case of beans, pasta, sawdust or salt you should use a thick paintbrush and varnish very slowly with plenty of varnish, dabbing it on softly rather than stroking the brush along. Sometimes it will be necessary to ask an adult to help.

Methodological guidelines

Based on our own professional experience in early childhood Education, we suggest what could be a good methodological approach for carrying out artistic activities in the classroom with children of these ages. The most important thing is to plan the classroom, activity and the materials well. The teacher should know exactly what the materials will be necessary for each session and which process to follow leading up to introducing the children to the activity. Before beginning to handle the materials and do the task, the teacher should motivate the children so that they understand what they are going to do and why, so that in this way they are interested and motivated to do it. The teacher should motivate the children and situate them first in a suitable context for each subject matter, as a way of maximizing the educational aspect he or she wishes to elaborate. The child should understand that everything he or she does has a purpose, and could be used in other situations. This is why it is always important to consider reality before starting an activity. Once a child's curiosity and desire to discover things has been awoken, it will be time to show them what the work will look like when it is finished, with an example previously prepared by an adult.

One factor to take into account for achieving positive results is to choose the correct moment, and distribute the activity over various sessions. At this age children very quickly get tired of doing the same thing for too long, and for this reason, depending on the length and complexity of the activity, it should be done in more than one session. Depending on the number of boys and girls in the class, their character and characteristics (fidgety, distracted, quiet, etc) and the difficulty of the technique you want to use and whether it is the first time that they are introduced to it, you should work in larger or smaller groups.

When working in small groups, the rest of the children must by engaged in an activity that does not need the help of an adult, so that instead the adult can dedicate him or herself entirely to the small group.

If, on the other hand, you are working with a large group, the activity will inevitably be more directed and therefore the most important thing is to grab the attention of the whole group. Make sure you do not make the mistake of getting too involved in the child's work, and reducing his or her involvement. You should not be too worried about perfection but about how the child handles, experiments with and enjoys the different techniques and materials.

When doing an activity that children can perform alone, even when working in a large group, it is not necessary to direct them so much; it is more important that they should be able to express themselves freely. You should leave space for the child to be creative.

If the material you are going to use is very specific, give it out to each of the children, or place it in a container in the middle of each table so that they can all reach it easily. In this way you can reinforce the children's habit of sharing.

Most of the techniques shown with the different proposals in this book can be varied to suit different age groups.

This book has been designed to be a practical work tool, as it is based on our own real experiences. We hope that the guidelines and advice that can be found in it will aid and expand the task of teaching artistic expression. The way of approaching each task will help the work be more enjoyable and entertaining, so that both the child and the teacher will be able to enjoy it.

Organization of the book

This book is designed to be useful for the different age groups in early childhood education, and is classified according to the degree of difficulty of each activity. This classification has been developed by means of experimentation in the classroom with children of these ages, with whom all the activities have been carried out. It must be pointed out that this classification is purely a guideline, since the suggested activities are entirely open, and can be adapted to the specific needs of different groups.

This volume contains activities that are both flat and three-dimensional. Each activity shows the materials that are needed, the degree of difficulty (from one to three), the steps to follow to carry it out, and it is divided into the different sessions that will be needed. Besides, advice is given for making the most of the activity. Every step is accompanied by a photograph or illustration, to make it easier to understand.

Home and School

This book features activities that refer to a child's most immediate environment: home and school. Children learn about these two subjects as soon as they start school. In the case of the home, it is a starting point already familiar to them, making it easier for them to relate to the subject. In the case of school, the subject helps them situate themselves in this new environment, where they will spend a great deal of time, as well as helping them to understand the different parts of the school and their function. These are the two environments in which children will spend most of their time, and it is important that they know them well. Both family and school environments are very important for the child. They provide a reference point and a starting point for new experiences. Starting from the child's own family environment, oral expression is encouraged, with group conversations and an interchange of personal experiences that will help children establish a closer relationship with their classmates and with their teacher. Consequently, the selection of activities that we suggest refer to perhaps the most significant elements of these environments, although certainly there are many others that could be added.

The question is to allow the child to be able to see where these elements fit in and what their purpose is. With some of the activities it is also possible to reinforce personal hygiene habits, eating habits, the prevention of possible domestic accidents, as well as to encourage the development of personal autonomy and skills for playing and learning.

The activities relating to the home are: the range, the shower, the armchair, the washing machine and the bed. There are also activities that differentiate between different types of houses depending on where they are found: the house in the mountains, the block of flats and the country house.

The activities that are related to school are: the backpack, the "tunnel," the pencil, the slide and the smock. There are also exercises that could refer both to the home or to school: the clock, the sink, the doll and the ball.

The clock is an activity aimed at five-year-olds, as this is the age at which they begin to learn to tell the time. But if you use it with younger children, it would be better to use it simply as an element around the house. The sink is an element common to both home and school, as it is present in both places. You could also make use of it to deal with personal hygiene habits. The doll and the ball are part of a child's games, and so can be found in both places.

activity 1 The Range

What do you need?
- Light brown cardboard
- Yellow and white chalks
- Black and brown plasticine
- Green finger paint
- Advertising brochures and leaflets
- Stick glue
- Scissors
- Punch and felt mat
- Varnish and paintbrush
- Template (see page 42)

How do you do it?
This activity can be done in four sessions of approximately half an hour each, working with the whole class at the same time. It is best to do the third session in small groups, to make it easier.

Session 1

Prepare for each child:
- A light brown cardboard with the outline of a range already drawn on it
- A white chalk and a yellow chalk

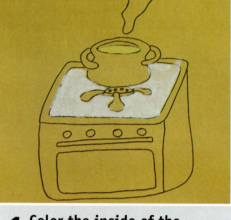

1 Color the inside of the pan with the yellow chalk to represent the soup and use the white chalk to color in the area around the hob.

Useful tips

- **Coloring with chalk.** When coloring with chalk, carefully blow on the picture from time to time, to remove the dust, so that it does not smudge it. Do not go over the area you have colored, because this makes the color lose intensity and dirties the area around it.
- **Plasticine.** It is best not to give out too much plasticine to the children so that they do not apply large amounts. The important thing is that with a small amount they can cover the whole area, spreading it in a thin layer. The children should wash their hands after using black plasticine, to prevent getting the paper dirty.
- **Varnishing.** Do not pour out very much varnish, as the area that has to be varnished is very small. As the children finish shaping the plasticine, let them go to the table where the varnish is to finish the session.
- **Printing with paint.** Try to ensure that the paint is not too liquid, so that when they print it with their fingers it covers the control knob properly with green paint.
- **Painting in with paint.** Use a very fine paintbrush and be careful that the paint does not go over the limits, as the space is very narrow.
- **Cutting out magazines.** Look for a picture that is big enough to fill the whole area of the oven.

What techniques do you use?

- Punching cardboard
- Coloring with chalks
- Modeling plasticine
- Printing and painting with paint
- Cutting out and sticking photographs from magazines
- Varnishing

Session 2

Prepare for each child:
- The light brown cardboard already colored in with chalks
- Black and brown plasticine

Prepare a table in one corner with:
- A container with varnish
- A paintbrush for each child

2 Use your thumb to spread the brown plasticine over the pan, and spread the black plasticine to make smoke and the hob. Then varnish it.

Session 3

Prepare a table in one corner (for 4 or 5 children) with:
- The light brown cardboard with the work completed in the previous session
- A container with green finger paint
- A paintbrush for each child

3 Use your finger to print the control knobs with green paint, and use the paintbrush to paint round the outline of the range and along the bar above the oven.

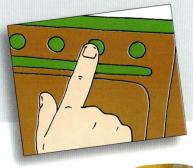

Session 4

Prepare for each child:
- The light brown cardboard with the work completed in the previous session
- Advertising brochures or leaflets
- Punch and felt mat
- Scissors
- Stick glue

4 Punch the oven door along three sides, leaving the left hand side whole so that the door is still attached and can open up.

5 Look in the advertising brochures or leaflets for pictures of food that can be cooked in an oven.

6 Stick the image you have cut out to the back of the cardboard so that you can see it when you open the oven.

Educational guidelines

- Work on **controlling the brushstroke** when varnishing and especially when painting with the paintbrush, so that it does not go over the line.
- Use the chalk on a surface other than the blackboard.
- Talk about **food** that comes from animals or plants, and comment whether it can be fried or cooked in the oven, etc.
- Discuss the possible dangers there might be in the **kitchen**, and about the precautions that should be taken to prevent accidents.
- Talk about the different **types of soup** they have tried.
- Reinforce their **fine motor skills** by modeling the plasticine.

activity **2** # The Slide

What do you need?
- A sheet of pink cardboard
- Black and white plastic crayons
- Blue glossy paper
- Yellow, orange and brown plasticine
- Stick glue
- Scissors
- Templates (see page 43)

How do you do it?
This activity can be done in three sessions of approximately half an hour each. You can work with the whole class at the same time, as it is a task that can be easily directed.

Session 1

Prepare for each child:
- A pink cardboard with the outline of an elephant already drawn on it
- A black and a white plastic crayon
- Blue glossy paper
- Stick glue
- Scissors

1 Use the plastic crayons to color the eye black and the tusk white.

2 Cut the blue glossy paper into fairly small pieces.

3 Spread the glue on the ladder, and on the elephant's cheek and ear and stick the small pieces of blue glossy paper onto these areas as a mosaic.

Useful tips

- **Making mosaics.** For sticking on small pieces of glossy paper, it is better to spread the glue onto the cardboard first and then put the paper in place to make the mosaic.
- **Cutting out glossy paper.** Depending on the age of the children you are working with, you can give them the glossy paper already cut into pieces, or you can let them cut it up themselves.
- **Balls of plasticine.** The balls of plasticine can be stuck on with glue, pressing gently to make sure they adhere better.

What techniques do you use?

- Cutting up glossy paper
- Coloring with plastic crayons
- Modeling and sticking plasticine
- Sticking glossy paper

Session 2

Prepare for each child:
- The cardboard with the work from the first session
- Glossy paper already cut into small pieces
- Stick glue

4 Spread the glue over the rest of the slide and stick on bits of glossy paper as a mosaic. The glossy paper should be placed with the blue glossy side down, to show the light blue side.

Educational guidelines

- Talk about how a **slide** is used for playing and having fun, and talk about the places where you can find one.
- Work on **psychomotor skills** on the slide in the playground, going up and down the stairs and sliding down the slide.
- Talk about **different types of slides** that you can find, depending on their size, color, etc.

Session 3

Prepare for each child:
- The cardboard with the work from the previous sessions
- A blob of yellow, orange and brown plasticine
- Stick glue

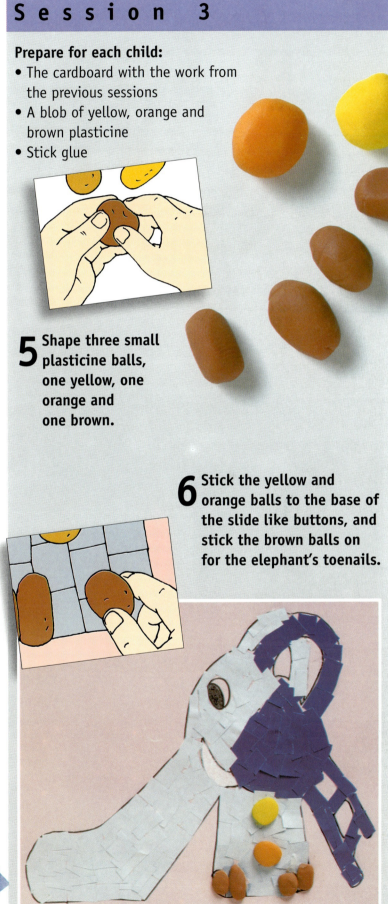

5 Shape three small plasticine balls, one yellow, one orange and one brown.

6 Stick the yellow and orange balls to the base of the slide like buttons, and stick the brown balls on for the elephant's toenails.

11

activity 3 — The Bed

What do you need?
- Pink cardboard
- Yellow glossy paper
- Blue crepe paper
- Thick red and blue felt-tipped pens
- Blue, brown and yellow plastic crayons
- Punch and felt mat
- Stick glue

How do you do it?
This activity can be done in three sessions of approximately half an hour each, working with the whole class.

Session 1

Prepare for each child:
- A pink cardboard with the outline of a bed already drawn on it
- Plastic crayons of different colors

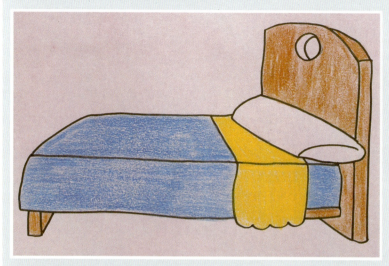

1 Color the bed with the plastic crayons, using any colors you like.

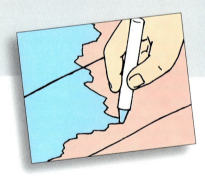

Useful tips
- **Making the pillow.** You can put your fingers up through the hole behind the pillow to make the pillow stick out a little to make it look cushioned.
- **Making dots with felt-tipped pens.** It is a good idea to warn the children not to press too hard with the felt-tipped pen, so that the point does not get pushed in.

Educational guidelines
- Show the children how to **make a bed** by means of a pretend game played in class.
- Teach them the vocabulary referring to the different pieces of bed linen that are used on a bed.
- Work on the **sensations** of heat and coolness that the bed linen we use gives us, depending on whether it is winter or summer.

What techniques do you use?

- Coloring with plastic crayons
- Punching cardboard
- Making dots with a thick felt-tipped pen
- Sticking crepe paper
- Sticking glossy paper

Session 2

Prepare for each child:
- The pink cardboard with the bed from the previous session
- Stick glue
- Punch and felt mat

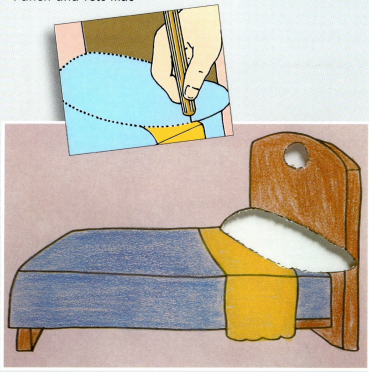

2 Punch and remove the pillow and the hole in the headboard.

Session 3

Prepare for each child:
- The pink cardboard with the work from the previous sessions
- A piece of blue crepe paper
- A piece of yellow glossy paper
- A thick red felt-tipped pen and another blue

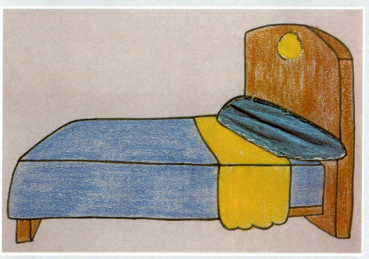

3 Glue the yellow glossy paper behind the hole in the headboard and glue the crepe paper behind the space for the pillow.

4 Make dots on the bedspread with the red felt-tipped pen and on the sheet with the blue one.

- Talk about the different **uses** for a bed: for sleeping at night, sometimes after lunch and when you are ill.
- Use the **felt-tipped pens** in a different way to usual. Making dots is a novelty for the children.
- Develop the **creativity** of the children by coloring in the bed as they like.

activity **4**

The Pencil

What do you need?

- A long cardboard tube (from kitchen roll)
- Yellow cardboard
- Yellow and green glossy paper
- A thick, black felt-tipped pen
- Adhesive tape
- Scissors
- Stick glue

How do you do it?

This activity can be done in three sessions of approximately half an hour each. You can work with the whole group at the same time.

Session 1

Prepare for each child:
- A yellow cardboard with the outline of the point of a pencil already drawn on it
- A piece of green glossy paper with a circle with tabs already drawn on it
- A thick, black felt-tipped pen
- Scissors

1 With the thick, black felt-tipped pen, color a corner of the shape on the yellow cardboard.

2 Cut along the outline of the shape on the yellow cardboard.

3 Cut out the circle on the green glossy paper with its tabs, and fold them so that they stand up.

Educational guidelines

- Talk about the correct way to hold **scissors** and practice cutting along straight lines and curves.
- Work on **mathematics** with a cylinder and a cone. Also work on the measurements of length with the strips of glossy paper.

What techniques do you use?

- Cutting out cardboard and glossy paper
- Coloring with felt-tipped pens
- Sticking cardboard and glossy paper
- Sticking with adhesive paper

Session 2

Prepare for each child:
- The work done in the previous session
- A long cardboard tube
- Adhesive tape
- Stick glue

4 Stick the ends of the yellow cardboard together with adhesive tape to make a cone that represents the point of the pencil.

5 Spread glue around one end of the cardboard tube, and fit the point of the pencil onto it.

6 Glue the green circle onto the other end using the tabs.

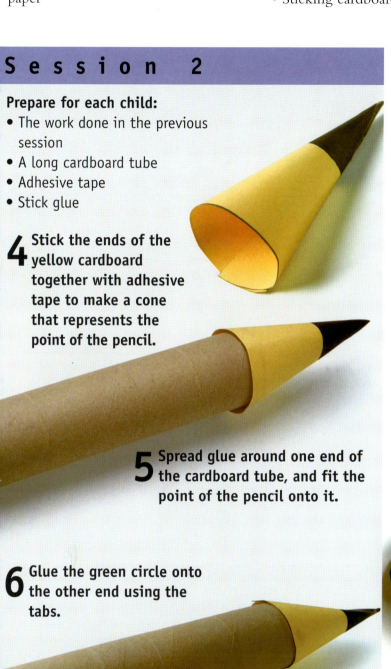

Session 3

Prepare for each child:
- The work done in the previous sessions
- Strips of yellow and green glossy paper (4 cm wide and 23 cm long, depending on the length of the tube)
- Stick glue

7 Spread the glue onto the strips of glossy paper and stick them onto the cardboard tube, alternating the colors yellow and green.

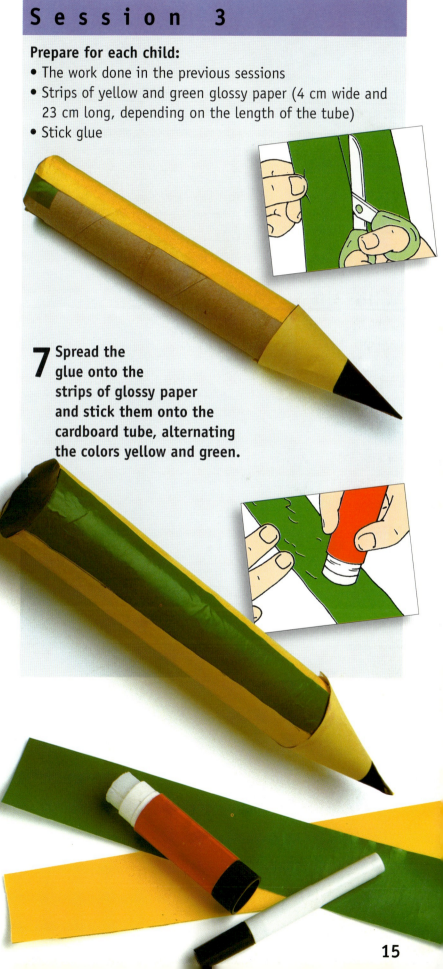

Useful tips

- **Making the task easier.** If you are working with younger children, you can make the task easier by painting the cardboard tube with finger paint instead of covering it with glossy paper. However, if you want to cover it, you can also do this by sticking strips of paper around the tube in circles (the length should be the same as the diameter of the tube).
- **Cutting out.** With younger children, instead of cutting out the glossy paper, they could also punch it.

activity **5** # The Clock

What do you need?

- A purple cardboard
- Small, round yellow stickers
- Gold, glossy cardboard
- Salt
- Colored chalks
- Sheets of paper
- Fasteners
- Punch and felt mat
- Stick glue
- Scissors

How do you do it?

This activity can be done in three sessions of approximately half an hour each, working with the whole class together.

Session 1

Prepare for each child:
- A purple cardboard with the outline of a clock already drawn on it
- Small, round yellow stickers

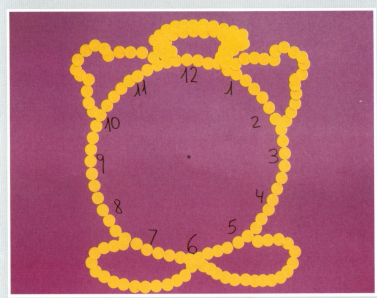

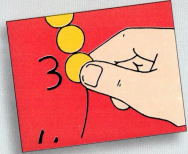

1 Stick the adhesives around the outline and handle of the clock.

Useful tips

- **Sticking on stickers.** If necessary, you should lay the stickers over one another so that the black line of the outline cannot be seen.
- **Sticking on salt.** To stick on the salt, first spread plenty of glue onto the cardboard, then sprinkle handfuls of salt over the top of it and press gently to make sure it sticks. Then lift up the cardboard over the tray to get rid of the surplus salt.
- **Coloring salt.** To color the salt it is best to give each child a sheet of paper and pour a little salt onto it. They can then color it until you have enough, making sure it does not spill off the sheet of paper.

What techniques do you use?

- Sticking stickers
- Coloring and sticking on salt
- Cutting out cardboard
- Punching cardboard

Session 2

Prepare for each child:
- The purple cardboard with the stickers stuck onto it
- Sheets of paper
- Blue and green chalk
- Stick glue

Prepare for each table:
- A tray of salt
- An empty tray for each color you are going to color the salt

2 Spread the salt over the sheets of paper for each child to color using the colored chalk until it has reached the required color. Each color should be put in a different tray.

3 Stick on the salt by spreading it gently with the fingers: green for the feet and blue for the bells.

Session 3

Prepare for each child:
- The cardboard with the stickers and salt already stuck on it
- A piece of gold, glossy cardboard, with the two hands of the clock already drawn on it
  - Fasteners
  - A punch and felt mat
  - Scissors

4 Cut out the hands of the clock from the gold, glossy cardboard.

5 Punch the center of the clock and the two hands. Put the fastener in place by inserting it through the hand to attach all the elements together.

Educational guidelines

- Practice the **numbers** up to twelve.
- Develop **fine motor skills** when removing and placing the stickers on the marked line.
- Work with the time **"o' clock"** looking at the small hand to see what time it shows.
- Use **salt** for something other than its habitual use.
- Learn to **color salt** for later use for other activities.

activity **6** # The Shower

What do you need?

- Yellow cardboard
- Brown wax crayons
- An orange plastic bag
- Blue cellophane paper
- Pieces of fabric
- Aluminum foil
- Blue tissue paper
- Stick glue
- Punch and felt mat
- Varnish and paintbrush
- Scissors
- Template (see page 43)

How do you do it?

This activity can be done in three sessions of approximately half an hour each, working with the whole class together.

Session 1

Prepare for each child:
- A yellow cardboard with the shower already drawn on it
- Blue cellophane paper
- Brown wax crayons
- Varnish and paintbrush
- Punch and felt mat
- Stick glue

1 Punch and remove the base of the shower.

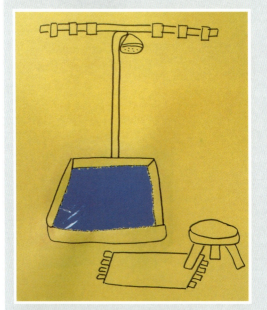

2 Stick the blue cellophane paper to the back of the yellow cardboard like a window, to look like water.

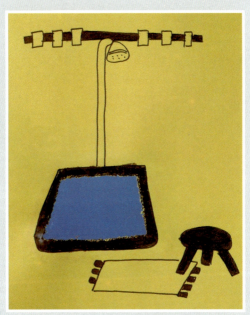

3 Color the stool, the fringe of the carpet, the curtain rail and the edge of the shower base, all with brown wax crayon. Then varnish them.

Useful tips

- **Sticking on pieces of fabric.** To stick the pieces of fabric onto the carpet, first you should spread plenty of glue onto the cardboard and then place the pieces of fabric onto it. If necessary, you will have to superimpose them so that they cover the whole carpet, filling in the edges first.
- **Sticking on aluminum foil and plastic.** It is best to give the children a long strip of aluminum foil and plastic, cut to the correct width, so that they only have to stick the top on and cut off what is left over.

What techniques do you use?
- Punching cardboard
- Coloring with wax crayons
- Making a window with cellophane paper
- Cutting and sticking fabric and aluminum foil
- Cutting and sticking plastic
- Rolling and sticking tissue paper
- Varnishing wax crayon

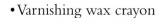

Session 2

Prepare for each child:
- The yellow cardboard with the work from the previous session
- A piece of fabric
- Aluminum foil
- Stick glue
- Scissors

4 Cut up the fabric into small pieces and stick them onto the carpet.

5 Cut out the aluminum foil and stick it onto the shower pipe and the curtain rail.

- **Varnish.** A container with varnish and a paintbrush for each child will be placed in each table, so that when children finish painting their work, they can varnish it.

Educational guidelines
- Work with **personal hygiene habits**.
- Develop **fine motor skills** when coloring and varnishing small spaces.
- Encourage the **distribution of space** when cutting out paper needed for a particular area.
- Work on the **shape of a rectangle**.

Session 3

Prepare for each child:
- The yellow cardboard with the work from the previous sessions
- Blue tissue paper
- A piece of an orange plastic bag
- Stick glue
- Scissors

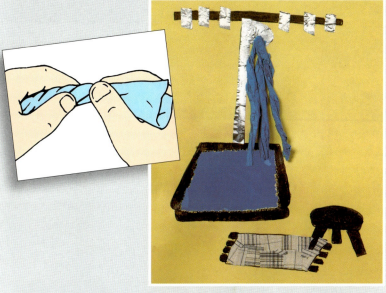

6 Tear the blue tissue paper into three pieces and roll them up to make "sausages" then stick them to the shower head so that they look like water.

7 Cut up the strips of orange plastic for the curtain, and stick them on at the top only.

activity 7

The Backpack

What do you need?

- Yellow cardboard
- Green wax crayons
- Black, brown, white and blue tissue paper
- Brown finger paint
- A wine cork
- Stick glue
- Varnish and a paintbrush
- Template (see page 44)

How do you do it?

This activity can be done in four sessions of approximately half an hour each. In the first three sessions you can work with the whole class together, but for the last session it is best to work in small groups.

Session 1

Prepare for each child:
- A yellow cardboard with the outline of a backpack already drawn on it
- Green wax crayons

Prepare a table in one corner with:
- A container with varnish
- A paintbrush for each child

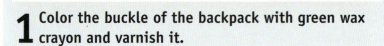

1 Color the buckle of the backpack with green wax crayon and varnish it.

Useful tips

- **Sticking on tissue paper.** When sticking on so many little balls of tissue paper, spread plenty of glue on the area where they are to go and then place them on it, making sure that the cardboard cannot be seen.
- **Varnishing.** Be careful not to dirty the yellow cardboard, and only varnish the area colored in. For this reason, it is very important to work with a very fine paintbrush.
- **Printing.** When printing with the cork, you should press gently and make sure that the cork does not have too much paint on it, so as not to dirty the cardboard. For this reason, the paint should not be very thick. The picture will look better if the surface of the cardboard is well covered. If necessary you can lay the cork print marks over one another.
- **Painting corner.** It is a good idea for an adult to be in the corner where the children are printing their pictures, to keep an eye on them and give them advice.

What techniques do you use?

- Coloring with wax crayons
- Tearing and sticking tissue paper
- Printing paint with a cork
- Making and sticking balls of tissue paper
- Varnishing wax crayon

Session 2

Prepare for each child:
- The yellow cardboard with the buckle colored in
- Black tissue paper
- Brown tissue paper
- Stick glue

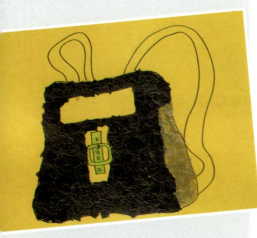

2 Tear the black tissue paper into pieces and stick them onto the backpack so that they cover the whole of the front part. Then do the same with the brown tissue paper to cover the side part.

Session 3

Prepare for each child:
- The yellow cardboard with the backpack already started in the previous sessions
- White tissue paper
- Blue tissue paper
- Stick glue

3 Make balls of white and blue tissue paper.

4 Stick the white and blue balls onto the central rectangular part of the backpack.

Session 4

Prepare a table in a corner (for 4 or 5 children) with:
- A container full of brown finger paint
- A wine cork for each child

5 Stamp the straps of the backpack with the cork dipped into the brown paint.

Educational guidelines

- Develop **fine motor skills** used in making a pincer with the finger and thumb for coloring, making balls of paper, tearing paper, etc.
- Talk about the functions and **uses** of a **backpack**, for going to school, etc.
- Group, compare and put into order the balls of paper that are left over (according to their size, color, etc.). Use the balls of paper to work on the concepts: **more than, fewer than, the same as**.
- Comment on the different uses of a **wine cork** and look at what kind of print it leaves (round ones).

activity **8**

The Washing Machine

What do you need?
- Blue cardboard
- Yellow glossy paper
- Yellow cellophane paper
- Red, blue, green and yellow felt-tipped pens
- Cuttings from advertising catalogues
- Scissors
- Punch and felt mat
- Stick glue
- Template (see page 44)

How do you do it?
This activity can be done in three sessions of approximately half an hour each, working with the whole class together.

Session 1

Prepare for each child:
- A blue cardboard with the outline of the washing machine already drawn on it (it is best to draw a square with a circle inside it)
- Different colored felt-tipped pens

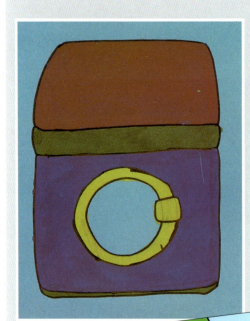

1 Color the washing machine with the felt-tipped pens, using any colors you want.

Educational guidelines
- Work on the children's **creative and artistic capacity** by letting them look for and organize the items they are going to use.
- Make **practical observations** about and evaluate the tasks around the home, emphasizing the collaboration of all members of the family.

What techniques do you use?

- Coloring with felt-tipped pens
- Cutting out cardboard
- Cutting out and sticking magazines
- Making windows with cellophane paper

Session 2

Prepare for each child:
- The cardboard with the washing machine already colored in
- A piece of yellow glossy paper
- A piece of yellow cellophane paper
- Punch and felt mat
- Stick glue

2 Punch and remove the circle that simulates the glass in the washing machine door.

3 Punch around the circle of the outside edge of the washing machine door, leaving a part unpunched.

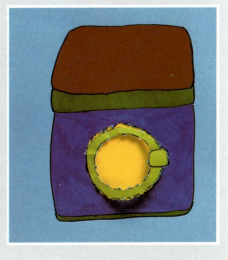

4 Glue the yellow cellophane paper to the back of the door, and glue the yellow glossy paper to the back of the cardboard, to look like the drum of the washing machine.

Session 3

Prepare for each child:
- The work that has already been completed
- Advertising brochures
- Stick glue

5 Stick on magazine clippings showing fabric, objects related to washing clothes, etc.

Useful tips

- **Magazine clippings.** It is a good idea to ask the children to collect the kind of advertising brochures that are normally posted through the letterbox. To gain time, leave them in a corner and let them cut out the ones they like in a free moment.
- **Sticking on clippings.** Spread the glue onto the back of the clipping, not onto the cardboard.

23

activity **9**

The Ball

What do you need?
- Green cardboard
- Small, round, white, yellow, red and blue stickers
- Black plastic crayons
- Template (see page 45)

How do you do it?
Being very straightforward, this activity can be done in two sessions of approximately half an hour each, working with the whole class together.

Session 1

Prepare for each child:
- A green cardboard with the outline of a ball already drawn on it
- Small, round, white, yellow, red and blue stickers
- Black plastic crayons

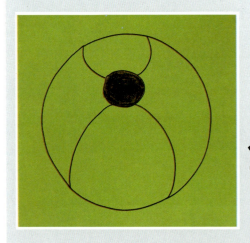

1 Color the circle in the middle of the ball with the black crayon.

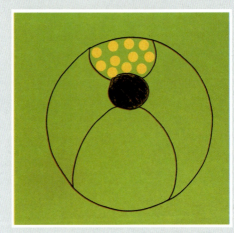

2 Stick the yellow stickers to the top part of the ball.

3 Stick the white stickers to one of the side areas of the ball.

What techniques do you use?
- Sticking on colored stickers
- Coloring with plastic crayons

Session 2

Prepare for each child:
- The green cardboard with the ball begun in the previous session
- Small, round, white, yellow, red and blue stickers

4 Stick the red stickers to one of the other areas of the ball.

5 Stick the blue stickers to the remaining area of the ball.

Useful tips

- **Sessions.** Despite the simplicity of this activity, the work is divided into two sessions so that the children do not get tired of sticking on stickers and in this way the result will be better. Even so, if you are working with older children, you could do it in a single session.

Educational guidelines

- Work with mathematics, using the **geometrical form** of the circle and the **location** of the different areas marked on the ball.
- Review **colors**.
- Develop **fine motor skills** by picking up the stickers with the fingers in a pincer position, and then sticking them down.
- Encourage the development of the **creativity** of the children by letting them choose the color of each area of the ball at their own will.

activity 10 The House in the Mountains

What do you need?

- Three pieces of cardboard in different colors: green, red and brown
- A square cardboard box (without the lid)
- Brown and white wax crayons
- White finger paint
- Lollipop sticks
- Stick glue
- White plasticine
- Scissors
- Paintbrush

How do you do it?

This activity can be done in three sessions of approximately half an hour each, working with the whole class together.

Session 1

Prepare for each child:
- A square cardboard box, not too big
- A brown wax crayon
- A red cardboard with rectangles already drawn on it, the right size for the box
- White finger paint
- Scissors
- Stick glue

1 Color the sides of the box with a brown wax crayon so that they look like the walls of a wooden house.

2 Cut out a rectangle out of a red cardboard and fold it in half to represent the roof. Stick it onto the box.

3 Print the roof with a finger dipped in white finger paint to look like snow falling.

Educational guidelines

- Talk about the characteristics of **houses in the mountains**: made of wood, and with sloping roofs to help the snow slide off.
- Think about possible questions like: What happens in spring when the sun melts all the **snow** that has fallen in the mountains? What happens in small mountain villages when a lot of snow falls? (Blocked roads, children can't go to school, etc.)
- Comment on the difference between **mountains** when they have snow on them and when they don't: landscape and use (for skiing or as pasture for animals).
- Think about typical **jobs** in mountain villages (wood cutters, forest rangers, etc.).

What techniques do you use?

- Cutting out and sticking cardboard
- Coloring with wax crayons on cardboard and on lollipop sticks
- Printing paint with your fingers
- Modeling plasticine

Session 2

Prepare for each child:
- A green cardboard with the outlines of two sides of a fir tree already drawn on it
- A lollipop stick
- Brown wax crayons
- White finger paint
- White plasticine
- Scissors
- Stick glue

4 Color the lollipop stick brown on both sides.

5 Cut out the two halves of the fir tree and stick the lollipop stick between them.

6 Print the fir tree with a finger dipped in white finger paint to look as if snow has fallen on it.

7 Shape a base of white plasticine and stick the fir tree in it so that it stands up straight.

Session 3

Prepare for each child:
- A brown cardboard with the outline of a mountain already drawn on it
- White wax crayons
- Scissors

8 Cut out the outline of the mountain, and paint the mountain tops with white wax crayons.

Useful tips

- **Sticking on the roof.** To stick on the roof, it is best to put plenty of glue along two edges of the red cardboard, bearing in mind that the part where the cardboard is folded has to be raised.
- **Gluing the fir trees.** First glue the lollipop stick to one of the sides of the fir tree, and then the other side, trying to make the two sides line up.
- **Gluing the mountains.** It is best to fold the lower part and stick it onto a base so that the mountain will stand up vertically.
- **Building a model.** Once you have made all the elements, they can be stuck onto a white wooden base to make a model which could stand on its own (three elements) or with others (with all the houses, trees and mountains of all the children).

activity 11 The Block of Flats

Session 1

Prepare for each child:
- A rectangular box (covered in white paper)
- Different colored felt-tipped pens

1 Using a black felt-tipped pen, draw in the different details of a block of flats: windows, door, balconies, etc.

2 Color the details of the block of flats with colored felt-tipped pens.

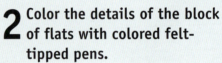

What do you need?
- A rectangular box covered in white paper
- Different colored felt-tipped pens
- Adhesive tape
- Black plasticine
- Round green, yellow and red stickers
- Stick glue

How do you do it?
This activity can be done in two sessions of approximately half an hour each, working with the whole class together.

Useful tips
- **Drawing.** Insist that the children think carefully about what they want to draw before beginning, as felt-tipped pen cannot be erased.
- **Modeling.** It would be easier to make the television antenna by beginning with the thicker, vertical pole and then adding the smaller horizontal ones.
- **Sticking on the antenna.** To stick the antenna onto the roof, squash the plasticine of the base a little with your finger, so that it sticks to the box, or reinforce it with glue.
- **Building a model.** With all the blocks of flats designed by each child, you could build a model of a town by sticking them onto a wooden base and complementing them with elements you find in a city (traffic lights, traffic signs, pedestrians, cars, trees, etc.) made from plasticine.

What techniques do you use?
- Coloring with felt-tipped pens
- Modeling plasticine
- Sticking adhesives

Session 2

Prepare for each child:
- The block of flats begun in the previous session
- Round green, yellow and red stickers
- Black plasticine

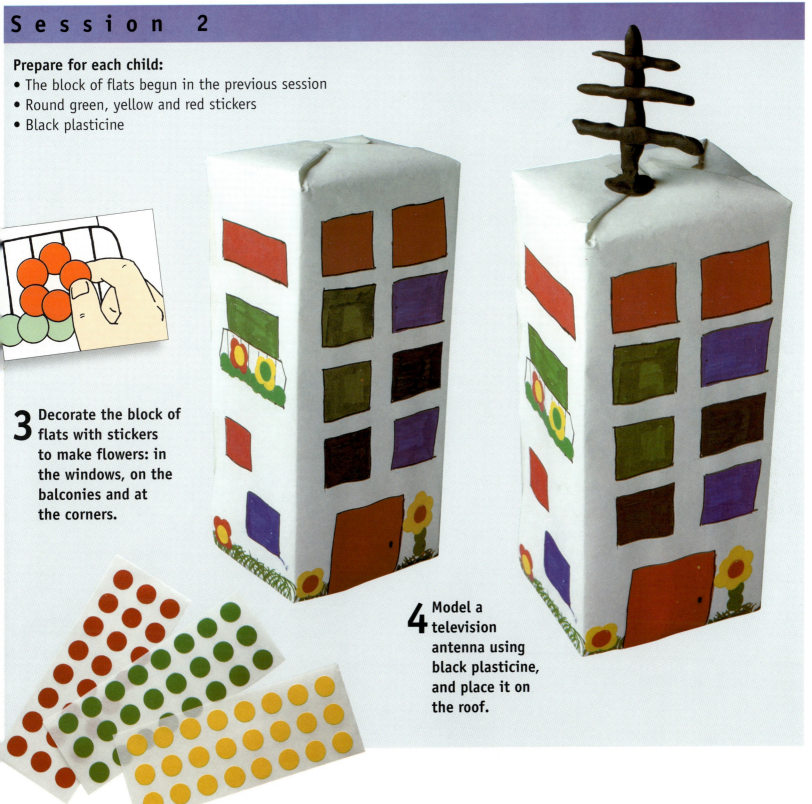

3 Decorate the block of flats with stickers to make flowers: in the windows, on the balconies and at the corners.

4 Model a television antenna using black plasticine, and place it on the roof.

Educational guidelines

- Talk about the differences between the shape of a single **house** and the shape of a **block of flats**. Why are there more blocks of flats than houses in a city? Talk about the differences between them.
- Encourage the development of the **creativity** of the children throughout the activity, leaving them free to design and decorate the block of flats as they like.
- Find out what the children have learned through **direct observation** of similar buildings in their own environment, in order to be able to draw a block of flats based on their own experience.

activity **12** # The Doll

What do you need?
- Yellow cardboard
- Brown, blue, orange, red and skin-colored plastic crayons
- Brown, orange and blue tissue paper
- Green crepe paper
- Small, round, red stickers
- Stick glue
- Template (see page 45)

How do you do it?
This activity can be done in two sessions of approximately half an hour each, working with the whole class together.

Session 1

Prepare for each child:
- A yellow cardboard with the outline of a doll already drawn on it
- Brown, orange, blue and skin-colored plastic crayons

1 Color the doll with plastic crayons, in any color you like, leaving the collar of the dress and the hair uncolored.

Useful tips
- **Tissue paper balls.** It is a good idea to put three trays on each table to hold the tissue paper balls, so that the colors do not get mixed up and to make the children's task easier.
- **Plastic crayons.** It is useful to remind the children that they should always color in the same direction, to cover the whole area and most of all to make sure they do not go over the lines.
- **Sticking.** Try not to get glue on the areas where you do not have to stick anything, since it makes the yellow cardboard go reddish.

What techniques do you use?

- Coloring with plastic crayons
- Sticking on stickers
- Making and sticking on tissue paper balls
- Creasing up crepe paper

Session 2

Prepare for each child:
- The yellow cardboard with the doll already painted on it
- Brown, orange and blue tissue paper
- Two small, round, red stickers
- A square piece of green crepe paper
- Stick glue

2 Stick the red stickers onto the buttons of the dress and crease up the center of the square of green crepe paper to make a bow, and glue it to the doll's head.

3 Make small balls of tissue paper in different colors.

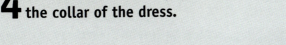

4 Glue the blue tissue paper balls around the collar of the dress.

5 Glue brown and orange tissue paper balls onto the doll's hair.

Educational guidelines

- Develop **fine motor skills** by having to make a pincer with finger and thumb to make the tissue paper balls and the bow.
- Talk about **parts of the body.**
- Work on **hair colors** (brown and orange) and their combinations.

31

activity 13 The Sink

What do you need?
- Orange cardboard
- Aluminum foil
- Blue tissue paper
- Blue rectangular stickers
- Gray plastic crayons
- White wax crayons
- Punch and felt mat
- Stick glue
- Varnish and paintbrush
- Template (see page 46)

How do you do it?
This activity can be done in two sessions of approximately half an hour each, working with the whole class together.

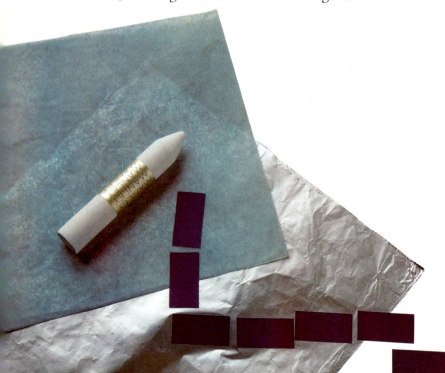

Session 1

Prepare for each child:
- An orange cardboard with the outline of a sink already drawn on it
- A white wax crayon
- A gray plastic crayon
- A paintbrush

Prepare for each table:
- A container with varnish

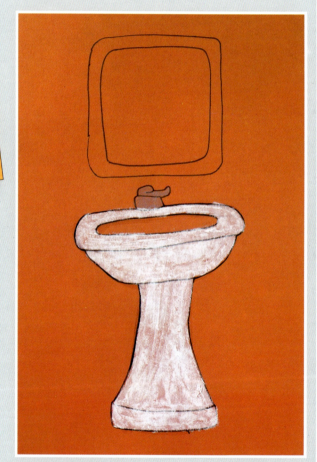

1 Color the sink with a white wax crayon and color the tap with a gray plastic crayon. Then varnish it and let it dry.

Educational guidelines
- Point out that a **sink** is an object found both at **home** and at **school**, but there are differences between the two types.
- Develop skills in handling different **materials** and using different **techniques.**

What techniques do you use?

- Punching cardboard
- Making windows with tissue paper and aluminum foil
- Coloring with plastic crayons
- Coloring with wax crayons
- Sticking on stickers

Session 2

Prepare for each child:
- The orange cardboard with the sink already colored in
- Aluminum foil
- Rectangular blue stickers
- Blue tissue paper
- Punch and felt mat
- Stick glue

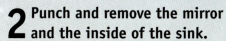

2 Punch and remove the mirror and the inside of the sink.

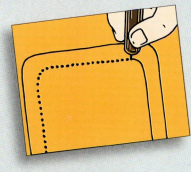

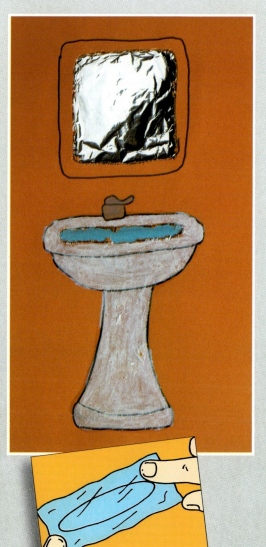

3 Stick the aluminum foil behind the mirror like a window, and do the same with the blue tissue paper behind the sink.

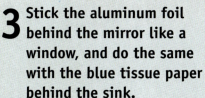

4 Stick the rectangular blue stickers around the mirror, like a mosaic.

Useful tips

- **Varnishing.** The work done in the first session is finished very quickly, but it is better to varnish it and let it dry before continuing with the following sessions, to ensure that the wax and plastic will not stain the cardboard.

activity **14** # The Smock

What do you need?

- Pink cardboard
- Red glossy paper
- Red wax crayons
- Red wool
- Punch and felt mat
- Stick glue
- Varnish and paintbrush
- Scissors
- Template (see page 46)

How do you do it?

This activity can be done in three sessions of approximately half an hour each. For the first two you can work with the whole group, but for the third is better to work in smaller groups to make the task easier.

Session 1

Prepare for each child:
- A pink cardboard with the outline of the smock already drawn on it
- Red glossy paper
- Punch and felt mat
- Stick glue

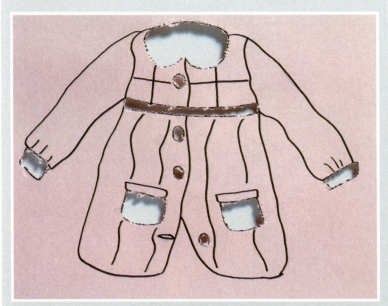

1 Punch and remove the neck, wristbands, buttons, pockets and breast band of the smock.

2 Glue the red glossy paper to the back of the cardboard to cover up the holes punched.

What techniques do you use?

- Coloring with wax crayons
- Punching cardboard
- Making windows with glossy paper
- Sticking on wool
- Varnishing

Session 2

Prepare for each child:
- The red cardboard with the work begun in the previous session
- A red wax crayon
- Varnish and a paintbrush

3 Using red wax crayon, color alternate squares on the smock and the pocket flaps. Then varnish them.

Session 3

Prepare for each child:
- The pink cardboard with the work from the previous sessions
- Red wool
- Scissors
- Stick glue

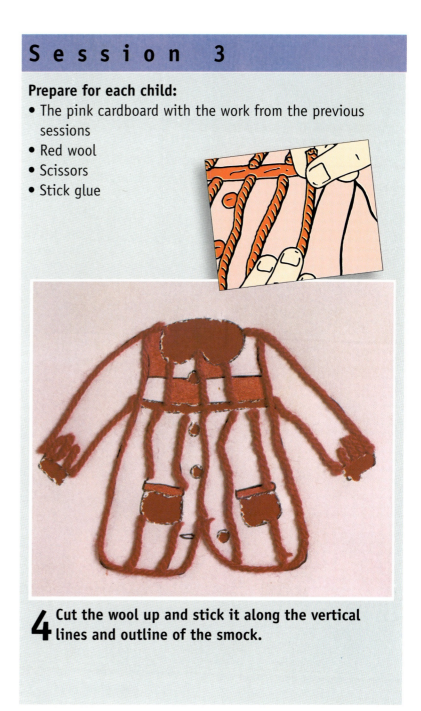

4 Cut the wool up and stick it along the vertical lines and outline of the smock.

Useful tips

- **Sticking glossy paper.** It would be more practical to give the children one large piece of glossy paper so that when they stick it on, it covers the whole drawing.
- **Sticking on wool.** To stick on the wool, spread glue along the line you want to cover and put the wool in place as you go along, until you get to the end, and then cut it.
- **Varnishing.** You should use a small paintbrush and a small quantity of varnish to cover just the squares you have colored in, without getting the rest dirty. It is useful to put a container full of varnish and paintbrushes on a table in one corner so that the children can go up to use it as they finish coloring in.

Educational guidelines

- Work with different types of **lines**: vertical, horizontal, straight and curved
- Talk about the diversity, uses and functions of **smock** (at school, in shops, in factories, etc.)
- Develop **fine motor skills** by controlling the brushstroke when coloring in small areas, punching and sticking on the wool.

activity 15 The Armchair

What do you need?
- Yellow cardboard
- Pink, dark blue and light blue wax crayons
- Yellow and blue finger paints
- A pencil
- Varnish and a paintbrush
- Template (see page 47)

How do you do it?
This activity can be done in two sessions of approximately half an hour each, working with the whole class together.

Session 1

Prepare for each child:
- A yellow cardboard with the outline of an armchair already drawn on it
- Pink, dark blue and light blue wax crayons
- A paintbrush

Prepare for each table:
- A container full of varnish

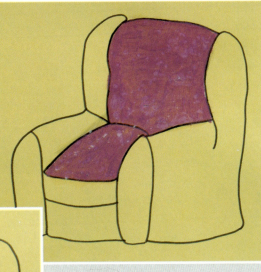

1 Color the cushion and the back of the armchair pink.

2 Color the front panels of the armchair with a dark blue crayon.

3 Color everything else using a light blue crayon. Varnish it and let it dry.

Educational guidelines
- Name **different items of furniture** that we use to sit on and rest on, as well as the materials they are made of.
- Work with the **concepts** related to the item of furniture: soft/hard, big/small, smooth/rough, etc.

What techniques do you use?
- Coloring with wax crayons
- Printing with paint

Session 2

Prepare for each child:
- The yellow cardboard with the armchair already colored in
- A pencil

Prepare for each table:
- One container full of blue finger paint, and another one full of yellow finger paint

4 Dip the flat end of the pencil into the yellow paint and print it onto the parts of the armchair that have been colored blue.

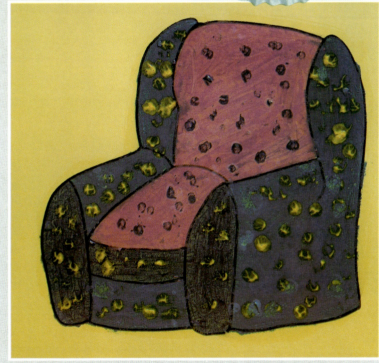

5 Dip the flat end of the pencil into the blue paint and print it onto the parts of the armchair that have been colored pink.

Useful tips
- **Coloring with wax crayons.** To prevent the children dirtying the cardboard with their hands as they color with wax crayons, it might be useful to use tracing paper, or any other type of paper, to rest the hand that is holding the cardboard on.
- **Printing.** To wash the paint off the pencil you are using for printing, it is very handy to use damp towels, so that the children do not have to keep getting up to go to the sink.

activity **16** # The "Tunnel"

What do you need?
- Orange cardboard
- Black red, green and blue felt-tipped pens
- Red, yellow and green crepe paper
- Scissors
- Stick glue
- Template (see page 47)

How do you do it?
This activity can be done in two sessions of approximately half an hour each. You can work with the whole class together.

Session 1

Prepare for each child:
- An orange cardboard with the outline of the tube (tunnel) and the child already drawn on it
- Colored felt-tipped pens

1 Color the child inside the tube using felt-tipped pens, in any color you like.

Useful tips
- **Cutting out crepe paper.** It is better to give the children the pieces of crepe paper cut to the required length, so that they only have to cut them to the right width. Bear in mind that the strips should be double thickness, so that the drawing of the child does not show through.
- **Strips of crepe paper.** Give out enough strips of crepe paper of different colors so that the children can choose for themselves the colors they use, the order they stick them in, the number they want and the width they cut them to.
- **Sticking on the strips.** To double up the strips, first glue them along the top edge only, then fold them in half and stick the other end down.

What techniques do you use?
- Coloring with felt-tipped pens
- Cutting out crepe paper
- Sticking crepe paper

Session 2

Prepare for each child:
- The orange cardboard with the child already colored in
- Red, yellow and green crepe paper
- Scissors
- Stick glue

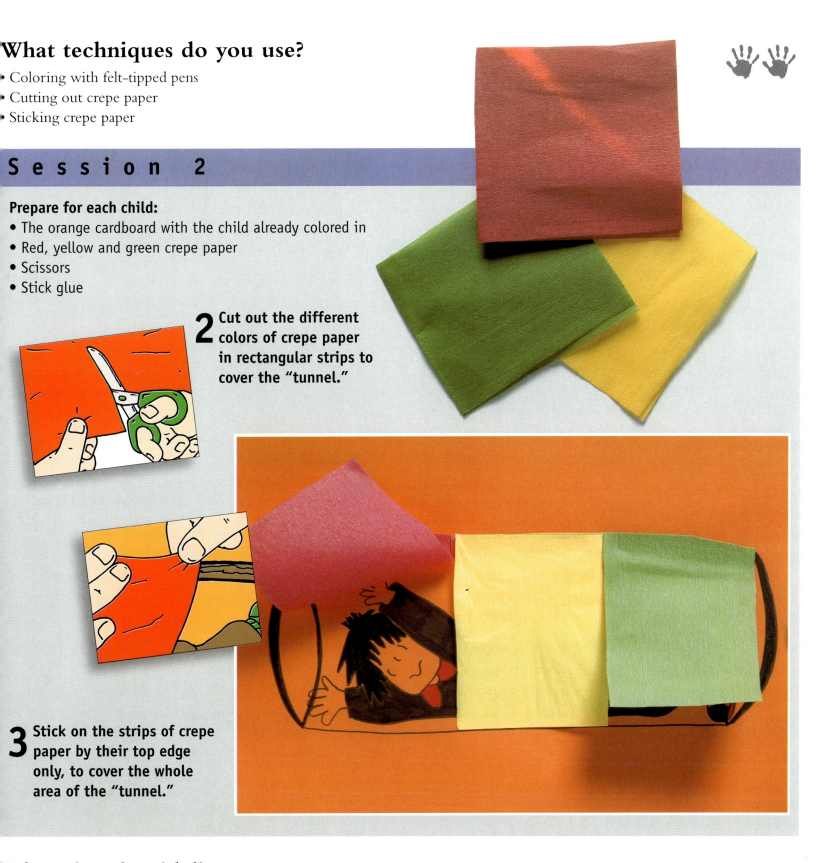

2 Cut out the different colors of crepe paper in rectangular strips to cover the "tunnel."

3 Stick on the strips of crepe paper by their top edge only, to cover the whole area of the "tunnel."

Educational guidelines

- Encourage the development of the children's **creativity** by letting them decide for themselves how they color in the figure, which colors they choose, the strips of crepe paper that they have to cut up and the order in which they stick these strips on.
- Work on the skill of **arranging** the strips of paper in a specific **space** (the tube or "tunnel"). They have to cut enough strips to cover the whole area.
- You can work with **parts of the body** and **laterality**, thinking about which part of the child's body you will see when you lift up just one of the strips of paper, depending on whether it is the one on the right, the left or in the middle.
- You can work with ordinal and cardinal numbers, following the instructions of the teacher: lift up the yellow strip first, lift up all three colors, etc. You can also reinforce **differentiation** of colors in this way.
- Work on mathematics by means of various concepts: the **middle** (when folding the cut strips before sticking them down), **wide/narrow** (different widths of paper strips), **more than, less than, the same as,** etc.

activity 17 The Country House

What do you need?
- Blue cardboard
- Red and yellow glossy paper
- Yellow cellophane paper
- Green tissue paper
- Small, round, blue stickers
- White wax crayons
- Stick glue
- Varnish and paintbrush
- Punch and felt mat
- Template (see page 48)

How do you do it?
This activity can be done in three sessions of approximately half an hour each, working with the whole class together.

Session 1

Prepare for each child:
- A blue cardboard with the outline of the house already drawn on it
- A white wax crayon
- Varnish and a paintbrush

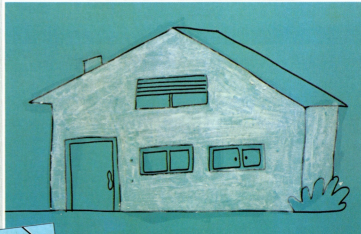

1 Color the walls of the house with a white wax crayon, leaving the windows and door blank. Then varnish the whole drawing.

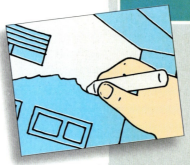
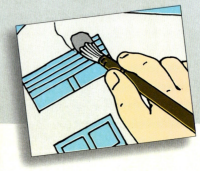

Useful tips

- **Making windows.** Spread the glue onto the cardboard and stick a large piece of yellow cellophane paper to cover up all the windows at the same time.
- **Coloring with wax crayons.** When coloring the house with white wax crayon, make sure the crayons are new, as they must be very clean to prevent them dirtying the picture.

Educational guidelines

- Talk about the different **types of home** that exist: single houses, village houses, flats, etc.
- Work on mathematics, **counting groups** of children who live in houses or in blocks of flats. Also work on **rectangular shapes**.

What techniques do you use?

- Tearing glossy paper
- Coloring with wax crayons
- Making and sticking on tissue paper balls
- Sticking glossy paper
- Making windows with glossy paper and cellophane
- Punching cardboard
- Sticking on stickers
- Varnishing

Session 2

Prepare for each child:
- The blue cardboard with the house colored in
- Yellow glossy paper
- Yellow cellophane paper
- Punch and felt mat
- Stick glue

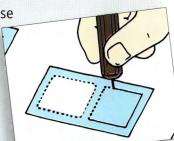

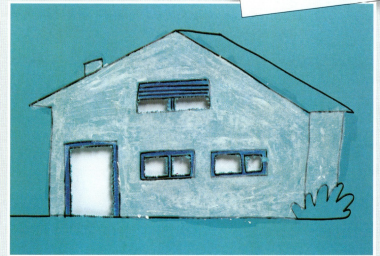

2 Punch and remove the door and windows.

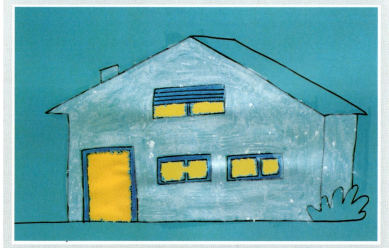

3 Stick a piece of yellow cellophane paper behind the windows, and stick a piece of yellow glossy paper behind the door.

- Talk about the different **textures** of the different types of paper you have used.
- Comment on the **distribution of space** (top/bottom) of the windows, doors, roof, garden, etc.

Session 3

Prepare for each child:
- The blue cardboard with the house begun in the previous sessions
- Red glossy paper
- Green tissue paper
- A small, round, blue sticker

4 With your fingers, tear the red glossy paper into pieces and stick them onto the roof of the house. Then stick the blue sticker on for the door handle.

5 Make balls of green tissue paper and stick them onto the sides of the house to look like plants.

TEMPLATES

What do you need?
- Tracing paper
- Black felt-tipped pens
- Carbon paper or a photocopier

How do you do it?
Trace the template onto the tracing paper with the felt-tipped pen. Then photocopy the result onto the color of cardboard you have chosen. If you do not have a photocopier, go over it using carbon paper.

Activity 1

Activity 2

Activity 6

43

TEMPLATES

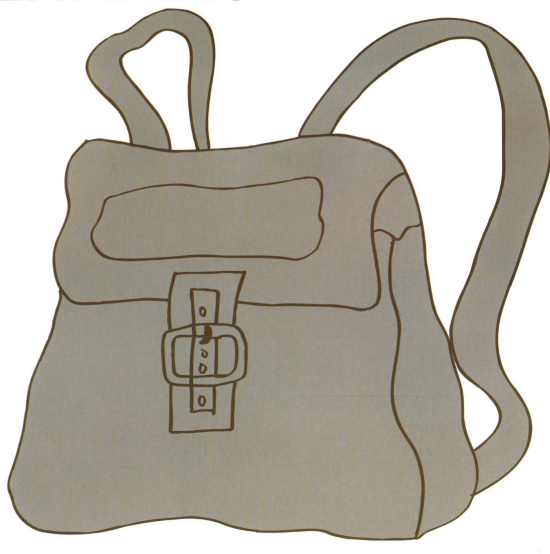

Activity 7

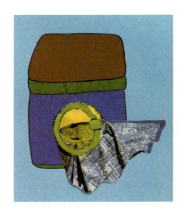

Activity 8

Activity 9

Activity 12

45

TEMPLATES

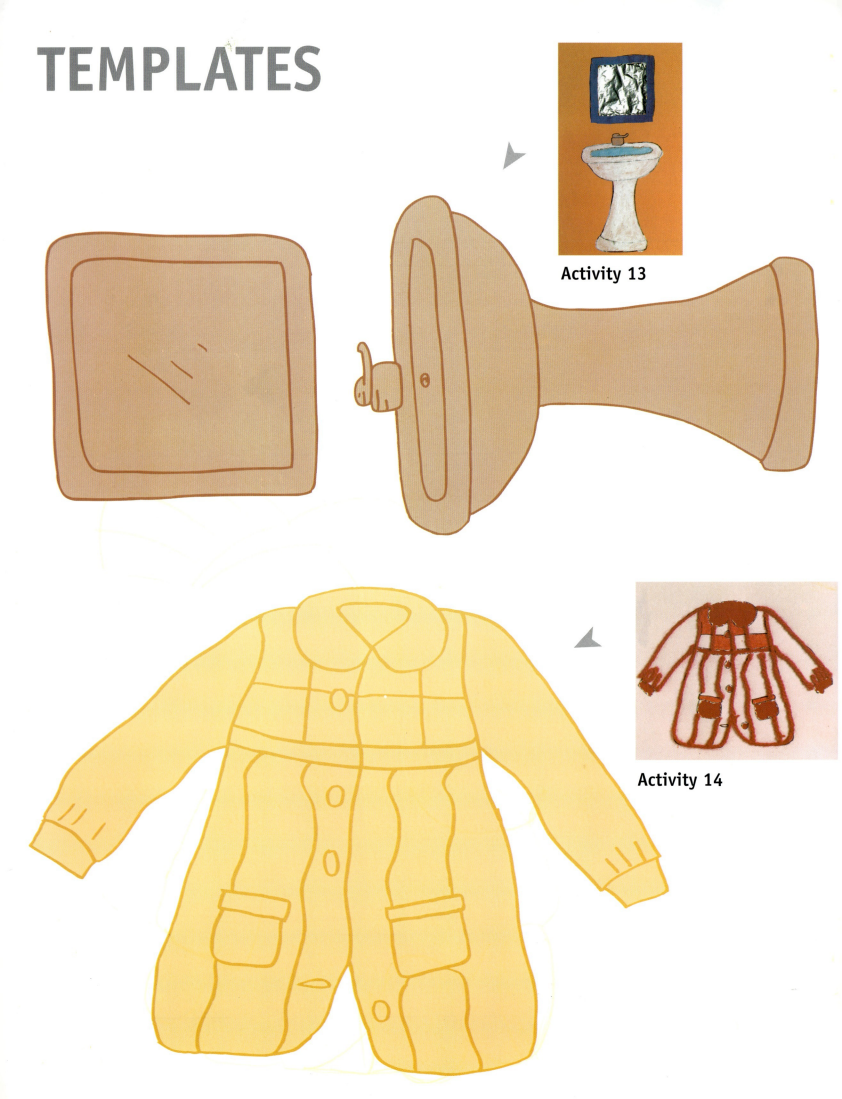

Activity 13

Activity 14

Activity 15

Activity 16

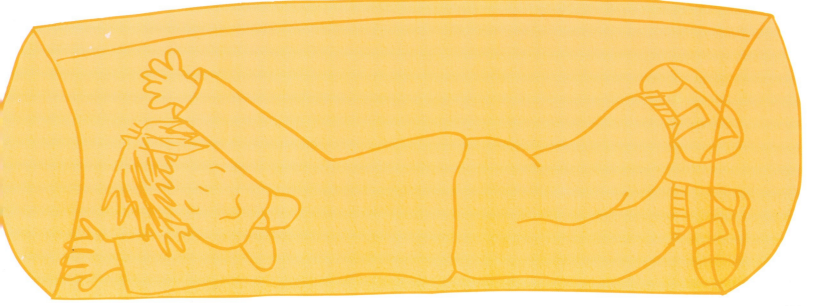

TEMPLATES

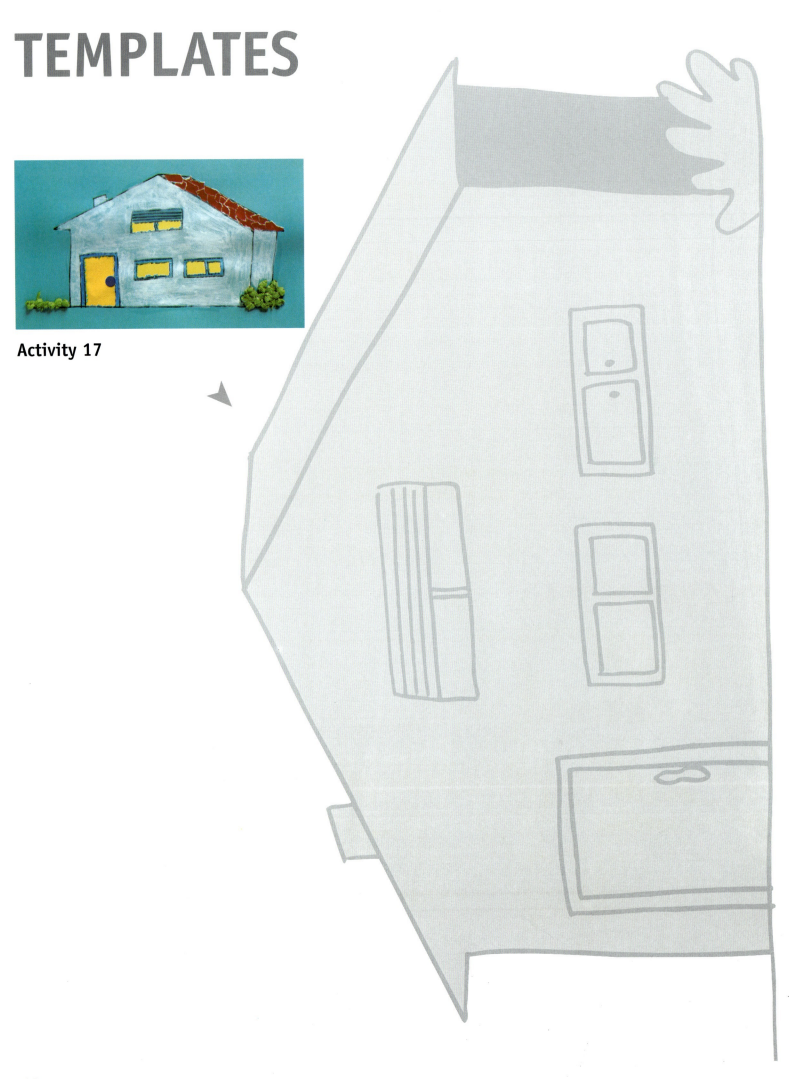

Activity 17